HHB

Bringing
a Fir Straight
Down

Poems by

Hugh Ogden

For Fred, whose skill in basketball was an art all to its own Love Hugh

HHB

Higganum Hill Books : Higganum, Connecticut

First Edition
First Printing May 1, 2005

Higganum Hill Books
P.O. Box 666, Higganum, CT 06441
Phone (860) 345-4103
Email: rcdebold@mindspring.com

Library of Congress Control Number 2004021153
ISBN: 0-9741158-3-5
Cover Painting: A detail from *Harbinger* by Virginia Dehn.
©2004   All rights reserved. Used by Permission.
The Photograph of the suthor is by Nick Lacy
©2004   All rights reserved. Used by permission.

Library of Congress Cataloging-in-Publication Data

Ogden, Hugh, 1937-
  Bringing a fir straight down : poems / byHugh Ogden.-- 1st ed.
    p. cm.
  ISBN 0-9741158-3-5 (alk. paper)
  I. Title.
  PS3565.G383B75 2005
  811'.54--dc22
                              2004021153

Independent Publishers Group distributes Higganum Hill Books.
Phone: (800) 888-4741   www.ipgbook.com
Printed in the United States of America.

ACKNOWLEDGEMENTS:

Some of theses poems appeared in the following periodicals and anthologies, often in earlier versions:

THE CHRISTIAN CENTURY, THE CONNECTICUT REVIEW, CONNOTATIONS, THE COMMON GROUND REVIEW, FOLIO, THE FOURTH RIVER: NATURE & CULTURE, THE FRANK WATERS FOUNDATION NEWSLETTER, FRESH WATER: POEMS FROM THE RIVERS, LAKES AND STREAMS (ed. Jennifer Bosveld), THE GREAT AMERICAN POETRY SHOW, THE LOUISVILLE REVIEW, LYNX EYE, THE MALAHAT REVIEW, NIMROD, NORTH DAKOTA QUARTERLY, PATERSON LITERARY REVIEW, PINYON POETRY, RATTLE, RIVER OAK REVIEW, SMALL POND MAGAZINE, SEPTEMBER 11, 2001: AMERICAN WRITERS RESPOND (ed. William Heyen), SOUTH DAKOTA REVIEW, SOUTHWEST REVIEW.

My grateful thanks to The Island Institute, The MacDowell Colony, The Ucross Foundation, The Frank Waters Foundation, and Fondation Ledig-Rowohlt (The Château de Lavigny) for Artist Residencies; to The Connecticut Commission On The Arts for a Fellowship Grant; to Trinity College and Dean Miller Brown for a Sabbatical and Research Leave; to Herman Asarnow, Arthur Feinsod, Emily Holcombe, Susan Kinsolving, and David Ray who helped me with these poems, and to Steve Foley for his years of help and guidance in writing poems (I know of no one who knows more about the making of a poem).

I also want to recognize two outstanding American artists: the painter Virginia Dehn (a detail from her painting, "Harbinger," is the cover for this book) and the sculptor Bill Burk (reproductions of his sculpture appeared on the cover of two of my earlier books).

CONTENTS

I

The Wide Space Of The Timbered Valleys

II

From The Connecticut To A Muskeg-Brown Waterfall

III

The Green Flooded Hollows Of This Mesa

IV

In This Vault

– for Kathryn, my abiding love
You make everything possible –

Bones are curved, and blood
travels a road that comes back
to that hill in my heart.

– John Haines –

I

The Wide Space Of The Timbered Valleys

Northwest Maine, September, 2001

It was a wide water day with the lake at peace
    and the wind

revising September-end-of-summer shore waves
    and it was

the silence of the wood stove percolating and
    then it was

the wake-up call on the air waves, the break,
    the interruption

of the Brahms symphony by a bulletin slipped in
    after trumpets

and violins were suddenly silent and it was
    the beginning

of what has always been the ending of quiet water:
    a voice

saying a plane had crashed into the North World
    Trade Tower

at the end of pure harmonies, flames replacing
    music

until the radio was awash with fear and bafflement
    and quickly

terror that thousands were dying, had died and then
    a second bulletin

that Washington had been bombed, a second plane
    had plunged

into the South Tower and I drove back down to
    southern

New England past the Androscoggin, the unfolding
    untouched

forests, the northern tip of the White Mountains,
    deep with

what the newscasters had left me, thanked the still
    green

translucent maples, the wide space of the timbered
    valleys,

the fact that my car radio was broken, the speeding
    season held

by road curves, river curves, in the drive down into
    the hurt

of what would become the everywhere broadcast
    of war.

Practicing For The Iraq War

Below the thunder of blue flame
thrusting two F-15s into purer
blue, the woodsman knocks snow

off gloved hands as he straps
on telephone pole climbing
spikes, shoulders a pull-rope

and climbs up the dead spruce by
the kitchen window, yells down
through snags and jet thunder

that he's an elf who can fell
the spruce exactly where he wants
it, secures the rope to the trunk

and rappels down, says elves in
his Cinderella story followed
the princess to the underworld

where she sought her husband,
returned limping with notches
in their glass heels. Then he

walks out on the frozen lake
to two snowmobiles chained end
to end and ties the rope, levers

it taut so the spruce bends
toward the sleds, returns to
the tree and chain-saws a mouth

on the fall-side as if notching
a glass heel, makes wood chips
sprinkle the snow like shattering

glass which none of us can survive,
then does a deeper face-cut so
tendons crack and finally snap

as an F-15 flies a fierce loop,
the other a boom-pinned-chasing-
turn over the spruce crashing

between saplings on the shore.
After the jets fly off through
blue, I think of how notches in

the elves' heels protected them,
of how frozen minds in Washington
have shattered like glass on

the skin of children, of the fairy
tale that's ended with our bombs
dropping on one of the cradles

we were born into and how all we
can do is what the woodsman does
as he walks out to the fallen crown,

the linked snowmobiles, stands in
his Xtra-Tufs as if he would grow
not just from earth, but from ice.

The Sound, Today, From The Palestine Hotel In Baghdad All The Way To Snow-Locked New Hampshire In April

After so much winter what is there to know,
days of wood smoke and fire,
days of radio listening,
pinned to the pain of the innocent
and to those who give it.
What is there to know?
I hold a news-photo of a turbaned old man in my heart.
I take him there, he will never leave.
I lift my eyes.
I rise into the simpleness of what is still around me:
hemlock, white pine, birch.
I walk to Baghdad in my dreams
I weep by the Tigris. I cry.
In the morning I write the first words,
like the first words written in Mesopotamia
centuries ago
with its fish, marsh-dwellers,
reeds twenty feet high.
Alexander never understood what he conquered.
Nebuchadnezzar, my God, Nebuchadnezzar.
And now George Bush and Saddam.
I bow my head and stand under all
we are capable of,
the least of it
a rocket blast on a hotel.
And an oak, an oak stands with me.

The Victor Manufacturing Company

Pigeons squawk high in steel-girdered
warehouse bays and Eddie punches

the computer as if pounding nails,
the option, control, but nothing

comes up right. A local comes in
to buy a gas refrigerator and he

rat-a-tat-tats the space bar with
his thumb just off the radio beat,

green fluorescence on aisles of
black pipe, gray propane tanks,

coiled copper tube, the business
just bought out by a conglomerate

and computer programs changed:
Eddie grumbles about memos, a CEO

swinging his chair and pushing
requisition forms, bird screech

through the bay, fat cylinders
hand-trucked to the loading dock,

the radio hip-hop beat interrupted
by news of B-52s over Kosovo,

a Stealth down, the generals
didn't figure the Serbs would hide

their radars or that Albanians
would flee into Macedonia. Eddie

goes on about the bastards,
the guys who run things, punches

a two with his forefinger, says
what it was like to get out of

the Ghetto in '68 and go to Nam,
the orders, flares, his eyes dark

as he starts to talk about his
buddy jacking canisters up to

plane wings before the mortar
blast but instead punches the two,

control, again and again, wing-
fluff of pigeons opening, the slick

grate of a bay-door sprung making
human lives invisible, keyboard

stuck, computer screen vivid with
wrong numbers, misplaced inventory.

Before Our Extinction

So what happened to the sequential
taking to flight of the loons
this autumn, this late November
when brown berries of mountain

ash turn red, turn outward in
migration toward new life, loons
south in their long straight
take-off lifting over winter to

Penobscot islands and the sea?
No flutter of pure piccolo where
before they would congregate in
song preparing to fly. They are

not here and I fear they will
never return when three geese
splatter a webbed take-off, making
me think of the shot-over-water

run of bones long evolved, not
from some hollow-boned ancestor
of the late Mesozoic, but from
a blood-drummed solid-boned

lizard whose feather-flute
haunts the air: they are not
here, are not, and who will
remember them when we are gone?

Night Driving

A man runs over a jack rabbit
which has run from a clear-
cut, drives on, turns around,
drives back, gets out, wraps

the dead rabbit in newspaper,
sees in its one opened eye
something calling without
sound and thinks – this is just

a rabbit, what's this about –
then puts the newspaper in
the station wagon. A partly
cloudy sky, three stars

around Saturn when he stops
on a grassy knoll by the bridge
over the Kennebago, carries
the newspaper to the snow-melt

flooded river, picks up a flat
limestone and digs, then puts
down this mystery he's been
part of, prays, kicks sand

over the hole to level the bar,
walks back into his dream, his
journey over road-crossings
under the witness of three stars

and a planet, a night sky he
knows he can't fathom, an eye
which sees and does not see,
buried by the river's deluge.

Buying Firewood

Buzz of a chain saw in
the wood yard as a grizzled
man and his son buck four-

foot logs, man-high pile
of splits in the hollow
between melting, dirt-

smudged snow banks. Greets
me with a wave, a tired
smile: fifty years married

and his wife with cancer
of the uterus, going down
to Rumford tomorrow for

chemo. He draws up the bed
daily after she passes
urine, feces. How much

a human contract matters.
The filth of our bodies that
someone's willing to clean.

That someone would stay by
us in the purple lost day
of our dying. On his door-

step, his knowing smile,
the sheen that masks
the lacquered grief that

13

covers plain ordinary pain.
Yes, he has firewood.
Yes, he'll deliver this

afternoon, get his son to
vigil his wife. Yes, his
open eyes that see every-

thing. We're silent, chain
saw stopped, a finch in
the gnarled apple tree

in the yard with only
the run of its first half-
melody, then our last words

as we turn to what needs
doing, wood for next winter,
love for what we have now.

What Sunday Means

Say maybe your three teen-age
kids have survived the cracked
years of the Twentieth Century,
that you were right in cutting
loose your husband of the last
decade, getting ordained and
finding a tiny congregation Down
East in Maine, say that in this
moment you're happy with your
new love, that you step in his
steps unto lake ice no more than
a week old with water pooling
far out as the ice shimmers
and creaks and you let that love
of yours lead on the Sunday
you have off because your kids
have flown three thousand miles
to their father in California
and a retired preacher is doing
the sermon, say you're happy
following where he walks as he
picks his way onto the frozen
surface but, when you step on
the same crack he's stepped on
and it snaps, your gasp over
all your hedged bets and every-
thing you can't control is
the harbinger of that panic-
cry when the next crack v-necks
and breaks so that his shoes
and pants sink and he's swinging

the oar he's carrying around
his head and down to the ice
in chest-high water and you're
on your stomach pulling that
oar and him back up, realizing
it's all luck, a blessing whose
grace slips towards you or
away because you can't be sure
early-winter ice will hold long
enough for you to reach shore.

Purging New Cylinders After A Two-Foot Snow

The gas man swerves his head
down to the TV when stock
cars scatter into sliding pile-

ups, then brings his face up
to tea and coffee as if rising
through water for air, relieved

and almost disappointed all
the drivers walked away, re-
joins us in the warmth of his

office-kitchen to talk round
what he wants sweet, what tart,
laughs to release a morning

swirl of mixed pleasure when
he remembers the tasty thrill
of driving a race track, how

he drove a three-ton truck
as a teenager and flirted with
blue flame by ratcheting hose-

valves or swinging levers open
to let propane flow and now
is back to an old career,

a business he'd not planned to
go into twenty years ago, what
he's seen of pile-ups, open

nozzles, explosions and, though
he's not an Ernhardt fan, he's
sorry about his death, about

any crash, then cuts more talk
with fire and tea in his cups
before stepping out the kitchen

door into knee-deep snow to
purge new cylinders until lemon-
rancid gas mists below-zero air.

Preservation

In an Adirondack chair on his front porch
the caretaker says the widow was a terror

in her last years when she executed her late
husband's wishes, set up a preserve over

hundreds of acres of lake-shore and woods.
He's logged since he was fifteen, knows

wilderness and pulp land and also knows
she created the preserve, even with her

high-handed, impossible demand that a fresh-
cut cedar be made the gutter and notched

to link with the over-hung rafters above
the office porch. She knew what she wanted.

When she crossed with him he went back to
felling trees, laying snares and traps,

until he had near let his anger run into
patience, into listening with the tips

of his teeth barely brushing his tongue
and then explained over and over you can't

put an outhouse close to shore, only need
a small office to run campsites, don't need

steps to get down to the lake. He held to
what he'd lived when she flowed up in her

black, rose-dotted skirt from the big city,
allowed her her words so a tiny wilderness

could flourish. He'd been born out near
Parmachenee and his hands carried the limits

of chain saws and trees, the civility
of brush-hogging a small plot to live on.

Etiology Of The Maine Woods

Trickle of a late summer brook
off South Bog Mountain, cinnamon
fir smell and the gate swung
closed on the logging road.

Then, over dirt ruts through
fir saplings and maple thick-
splurged in the old wood yard,
a Mead Paper 4x4 followed by

a Ryder truck and four more
4x4s all with three men who've
knocked-back raspberry and hard-
wood up the mountain, patrolled

to keep hikers at bay so they
wouldn't be hit by herbicide
their helicopter drops. With
the 'copter hovering above

the now opened gate and the last
4x4 through, the driver says
what's valuable are red spruce,
black, the fir, drawls to extend

meaning through the secrets
of a corporation, says knocking-
back kills raspberries and brush
so forest won't return to

hardwood, eyes birch and maple
inching up between bunch
grass, smiles with a knowing
smile as he grips the wheel

as if on a tractor plowing
corn fields, sits bolt still,
then presses the accelerator
so the truck tanks forward

under the down-rush of air
beaten by the 'copter, the clean
pungent wash of a mountain
brook under spinning wheels.

Steam Engine Placard Hanging
By The Driveway

Under heavy clouds and rain
a chain saw from across the lake,
then a pillar of black smoke:

the stock broker up from New
Jersey is having his timbered
land cut so he'll have all lawn,

a view to and beyond the lake.
Three years ago he had his
train-station house painted

gray so it would look like
what it was half a century ago,
had de-barked spruce trucked

to the water's edge to replace
rotten logs in the old steamboat
dock where overnighters from

Boston and New York stepped
down from sleepers and, with
safari hats and fishing poles,

bobbed away from descending
engine ash and walked with
porters and baggage to the boat

that ferried them to the hotel.
He was trying to be congruent
with antiques, trying to pretend

the past isn't past and now
– just like the sports who waved
their baggage to the boat – he's

in his black-striped, orange
blazer brokering his trees so he
can see and be seen in a cloudy

rise of a brush fire in rain.

Bringing A Fir Straight Down

Two black fantails float above
the knoll as the Wood's Boss

puts on his orange-muffler-
helmet, clips climbing spikes

to his boots and tells me
he lives with ravens to settle

his mind, pulls his gloves
off and shows me the walking

stick he'd carved 30 years
ago in the Smokies, says,

"raven's will is my will
and our wills are to survive,"

cradles it before he lets me
feel the worn, sweat-shine

grip of the carved raven's
bill, says, "they fly above me

on my long walkabouts from
'Hafen's Halla' to the bluff

looking over the Kennebago
where they cup-spread their

wings and tail-fans and land
beside my walking stick that

I lay down and point beyond
the river. Now watch them as I

drop this fir." Then he climbs
the trunk, chain saws the crown

in a flurry of wood chips,
ropes it easily to the ground

and the ravens gyre down, hop
about, croak, pick up wood

curls and lay them by the carved
raven-smooth bill, cluck their

certainty that their friend is
bringing the fir straight down.

A Huge Tract

Sweet, Crazy-Dave joined the Seventh-
Day Adventists and used a shotgun to
keep people off his eight-hundred feet
of lake frontage, his unlogged acres.

In town everybody thought he was mad
but he was serious: "No Hunting" signs,
"This Is Wildness," "Keep Out," nailed
every hundred feet along South Bog Road.

Hardly a soul ever saw him, especially
in winter when all of us thought
he lay down to sleep with his three
cows in the shed he called a barn.

When he died he had his ashes buried
in the poplar grove on the shore.
He wanted to be carried by roots
into the shimmering that leafs out

every spring, wanted the visibility
of rust-gold leaves in autumn after
the conflagration of the maples
just as he wanted to mark off with

his shotgun his diminished contact
with everything except trees and
cows: he wanted to signal wilderness
and the seasons of his own dimension.

Understanding

Clean, short-sleeved men in tan
shorts who want to look 'country'
stop at the country store for

fresh baked muffins and bagels,
stand around the backbed of
a shiny red 4x4, lean and sit

on the tailgate, angling their
heads low in whispers, raising
them like startled deer when

Saul drives up in his rusted,
black pickup with the backbed
taken off, Saul who's still

living in the shack his grand-
father pieced together ninety
years ago, a Chevy with no tires

in the yard, wheels and axles
sunk into what in mud-time is
mud, a bus with broken windows

beside the room he uses for
a bedroom, chickens pecking at
treadless ski mobiles, piles

of wooden pallets and back car-
seats, Saul, who waves his grease-
shadowed hand when he slides

out of his pickup leaving it
muffling with soft pops as he
limps up the steps for cigarettes.

The men in their shiny, flower-
blossomed shirts look at each
other and down at the shiny

red tailgate, baffled by how
anyone could still be living
with chickens when jobs are easy

and all you need do is stop for
morning coffee and a cinnamon-
glistening donut at the grocery.

Taking The Tent Down And Going Home

Alone as usual after the craft
fair, he asks her to bring the key-

hole to the painting table but
she goes on talking about how

only five tourists bought today
as she sits in the stuffing-broke

lounge chair in the workroom,
counts dollars, lists the fairs

they've gone to this summer where
they hawked oil-painted, used

ripblades, handsaws, scythes
decorated with roses, scarlet

bows, daffodils. He asks her
again and she goes on counting

so he walks to the workbench for
the keyhole he's salvaged from

the Collins homestead and, after
he's used emery paper, puts

the worn ground edge to his
chin and asks if she remembers

how he helped Abe cedar-plank
his boat, how Abe used his whet-

stone after a dozen blows so
he shanked a clean curl. She

says nothing, continues counting,
so he decides to use emerald-

green and blue to paint a trillium
on the thin blade, delighted

and absorbed by the fine-pointed
oil brush, the shape and color

the delicate flower will take in
the center of the keyhole, fragile

spring tendrils beside teeth
that will never be used again.

Circumference And Centers

Now that his wife's been dead a year,
Ray's got a savvy Doberman which
he's trained to make a circle when
she runs, a circle when she comes

to heel, a circle when she retrieves.
He claps his hands and Sweetie
comes out of her circles and sits.
Ray still has Betty's twenty-year-

old Cadillac and his own Chevy truck
and parks them in the garage under
the signs, "Betty," "Ray," and Sweetie
rides beside him when he drives

the Cadillac, raises her sleek
lynx head to watch the woods as
he talks about clouds and weather,
the two-foot snow that fell every

four days last winter. He drives
a big circle, returning to where
he started with Sweetie alert for
deer, rabbits, reaches into the glove

compartment for a biscuit when
she puts a paw on the brake, tells
her we always return as he pulls
under Betty's name in the garage.

Bending Steel

Burls of steel and scrap on
the machine shop floor as

Russell places the rear-door
hinge of a station wagon

on a steel plate, down-levers
the fifty-ton press with

his right hand and holds
the bent hinge steady with

his left. When he doesn't
get it straight he braces

it with a block and explains
the hardnesses of steel,

those that chip and break,
those that bend, how he

learned to work metal after
he got sick and had half

his stomach removed because
of a tumor. Asks me to pass

the spindle oil as he brings
the press down hard, with

muscle. His eyes a fierce
black halo. Says he's going

bear hunting this weekend,
clamp his soldered wire-

mesh, steel-rod hunting
stand to a tree and wait.

Bear season opens today.
He lifts the lever so that

the press sifts air, lets
go. He'll put jelly-smeared

bread and honey on a stump
and, when the bear comes

sniffing, rise with his bow,
pull the string to his lips

and twang a feather into
the warm black heart of bear

who will be nosing the bread
with a water-beaded snout,

his tongue pressing the taste
of death into an arrow.

Care

When you walk there it's
not the boards you feel

but your father's hands.
He'd hammered nails in

the beam that supports
them and the second floor

balcony of the A-Frame he
built years ago, tried

to flash the edges where
roll-roofing meets exposed

wood, what he knew and what
he didn't about building

a cabin on a tear-drop of
an island. But he missed

the rake-angle and the beam
decayed, the second floor

slanted so you'll have to
jack and replace it, redo

what he did when he built
in the lake to follow

the milky way or meditate
on round-the-lake views

floating the years around.
Come up every weekend

from the paper mill on
the Androscoggin, he wanted

to build to last, to leave
you an enduring cabin

as well as the lean-tos
in the bog to which you,

he, and your mother, boated
at dawn to watch heron,

moose, the osprey that
used to nest on the top of

a broken-off white pine.
He placed the A-Frame at

the water's edge beside two
birch and a hundred-year

pine, so when he stepped
out he stepped on a sliver

of ledge under trees, a
perfect match of cabin

and water. Now, when you
get out of bed and walk to

the balcony, you feel not
just the dreams and safety

of this house and the others
you grew up in, his hands

holding you and a hammer,
but the slant of his mistake.

Sweet Talk

Down at the gas station
three sweet-bellied men
have their feet up on
chairs, unlaced snow
boots beside the stove,
black wool hats pulled
down on their foreheads.
Touring ski-mobilers
come in, stumble around
the Jotul while the men
go on talking, eyebrows
barely visible, voices
low under the bob of
helmets, snowsuits, gloves
holding green to pay for
gas to ride the February
trails of high Maine.
The register never stops
clicking as the three
let their eyes rise, their
voices fall when Larry
talks about last night's
stove fire at the widow
Soule's that didn't get
much beyond the thimble
connector to the flue.
It was mostly him talking
the widow down as he sat
with her after they'd
vacuumed dry-chemical
fluff, sopped up puddles

of black water that had
poured from the red hose
they'd stuck down the pipe,
his voice sweet-low bent
irony laced with a smile.

Mountain Road Rally

If the racer's long gray hair
falls over his face '60s style
when he takes his helmet off

and inhales three times before
leaning against his red chess-
board-painted Escort, he's

just being the guy who drag
raced his Ford coupe down Main
Street forty years ago until

he heard the word 'Luv' and
drove off into the revolution.
He's doing what he's done so

many times, rev himself up
before he revs his stock car.
He holds his wife's hand, looks

at her deeply saying, "I feel
lucky, feel like we can match
any time and even beat it."

She's all smiles and dyed-hair
wrinkles with a beer bottle as
she bumps her helmet against

his, hugs him with a laugh
that carries over the mumble
of dozens of striped-yellow

or checkered-black painted
Lancers and Berettas lining
the mountain road, hugs him

like she did years ago in
the commune tent in the North
East Kingdom, curly black

hair hung to his shoulders.
Now she slides into the seat
next to him under her harness

and they drive up to the flag-
man at the logging road, then
in a rumble of muffler exhaust

and tires peal past yellow,
triangular heraldry pinned to
spruce and fir, race off over

rutted bumps with her leaning
sideways away from dusty turns
while he keeps the beat of

'The Grateful Dead' by glancing
at his Faith, shifts from
second to third to fourth on

tree-dense, dirt curves, spins
the wheel in mid-summer luck,
the holy dust of their lives.

Occurrences

Monday morning in March, fragile
thaw on the lake and the putter
of a ski mobile up the north

draw of the island. Spring almost
come out of winter as solitude
breaks, a voice, a guffaw, cartons

and shovels, sledge hammers, saws,
a work-day of clink and clack
and the whir of a drill — all's

normal in the woods, even the quiet
when Ernie and Matt take a breather
from framing and insulating a double

roof, gather around tools and sleds.
Thermos-coffee, a cigarette, as
Ernie says his two youngest took

their first snow-machine ride up
by Four Ponds over a crust that
allows access to every hollow, every

swamp. I've come to the mountains
for a week of sun-splashed snow
sliding into spring and to build

a five-foot fence to keep deer
from the garden. We go on, talk in
the normal sweet-greeting of people

who've survived, wet snow-pack
a blanched, stark glare with blue,
dark-green spruce and fir motionless

in the air of spring's first day,
this the twenty-first of March
when warmth comes through our

unzipped parkas just before Ernie
says it's the anniversary of his
oldest son's dying eleven years ago,

great gangling kid with buffed-
blond hair who lifted an engine
block out of a Nissan, squiggled

under it as the pulley slipped.
Oh, the running of season into
season, the fragileness of how

we talk about daily occurrences
in the wrench of our lives, in
the slippage of winter into spring.

Making The Day Endure

Sleepless again, I dream
of axing fir bark off
a stringer: It separates
with the slap of a fish-
tail as the blade goes
down wet length of de-
limbed trunk, living
flesh from which fir
grows its girth, out of
which it rises to new air.
The night closes the windows
of light and wind rinses
the room of bureau and desk.
When I slide a curved
drawshave under the bark,
pungent fir clings sweet
to steel and tree-skin
releases with a long kiss,
the moment of forgetting
the bed I am in, the night
I fall asleep through,
the stringer now perfected
in its oiled yellow shine.

Lake Freeze

Slow flicker of flame
   behind the wood stove

glass and the quiet of
   iron radiating warmth.

Outside, curtains of
   mist hang between shore

and island as water
   gives up heat to – 20

degree temperatures,
   an unmoving, buoyant

cloud-fog that seeps
   silently on to land

whitening cabins, fir,
   and spruce. Hoar frost.

Inside and out, trans-
   formation. Either snow-

mist or radiant invisi-
   bility, a cast iron

mirage of heat meeting
   window and wall, white

condensed lake-frost
   coating the shore, cabin

smoke rising into blue
   mirrored in heavy dark

water about to change to ice.

A Wild Sermon

Someplace in the anywhere
   nowhere world you'll bid
      hello, good-bye, as Jesus did

asking his friends to
   love one another – that's
      the Minister's text from *John*

under the four equilateral
   triangles of roof risen over
      the rough log church in the Maine

woods. He uses it to lead
   into his sermon about giving
      ourselves to lilac time, lupine,

any time in any season,
   even to the moment of departure,
      reads a psalm lifted from the desert

centuries ago, then,
   after the benediction, walks
      down the aisle to the door to shake

hands with everyone,
   sees the moose plunging
      his head in swamp-grass across

the road, points with
   his Bible at the swagging,
      dumb-struck, dripping-wet head

before the bull slogs
   over the culvert and lumbers
      towards mothers, fathers, kids

with cameras who back-
   peddle and stumble to escape
      the black-brown divinity trailing

green strands from lips
   and antlers, all of them
      wanting to see but not get too close

while the congregates
   stop bidding hello, good-bye,
      stunned by presence everywhere.

Lyric

In the sunlit lake there's
nothing but light, nothing

but sun-changed air changing
water, a summer's day, far

waves come near and close
in wind-rippled transparency,

dark surface turned blue, depth
of shore turned outward into

green, mountain ridge line
falling from on high into

cerulean, pool-sparkle of
waves so that everything

appears to disappear into
the whole, into circles of

sunlight opening, a vortex
of wind, water, and air from

around the globe leading
out of and into this world.

I say these words quietly
because this sun-lit lake is

folding into revelation as
light passes away in more light.

At The Millennium

Thanks be for the calendars that
    deflected the rock my back-side fell
        on, appointment books for '99 and 2000

in my pocket: I took only a sharp
    bruise there, not a broken hip, had
        a limp for seven days because days – no,

years, no, centuries – kept flesh
    from rupture, the purple splash only
        unfolding in less than a purple symmetry.

That's what the measure of time
    does when kept on the back end of
        my days, all those engagements, dates

taken out of my head and put on
    the year's pages, a little cushion
        to help when I step with a walking-stick

on rained-on lake ice, slip at
    the edge where rocks thrust up
        a pressure-ridge cracked from zero

temperatures. I feel melted ice
    soaking my pants lying there with
        hip on stone, not just hip but date

books, stunned clouds sliding over-
    head, months and numbers leafed to-
        gether on stone and ice this the first day

of a new century – no, millennium,
　　no, no – just a day in winter when
　　　the only thing moving is far-away sky.

II

From The Connecticut To A Muskeg-Brown Waterfall

On A Bluff Above The Connecticut

I see only floodplain
water far off and near,
willow and ash above
spring snow-melt, no
river channel, though
I can feel the current
from this plateau of
sand-loam soil, can
guess where the channel
is and where the creek
joins the flow down to
the sound and the ocean,
little pieces of yesterday
barely visible, barely
moving. It's so still on
a late March afternoon
and I'm someplace high
looking down. Tomorrow
I'll return, even if
wind and rain try my
legs and I can't see
the river, only a flood-
plain of spring runoff,
though I'll know by
feel where the channel
is as I do now, this
place I'm in, the flood
of it all, the stillness.

Listening At The Spring

Out through Cobalt and by
the Connecticut that cuts
the hills below Middletown,

up past new subdivisions,
old Victorians, to where Route
16 crests, then falls to

the Salmon, there's a recess
of hemlocks where you can
back in your car filled with

empty bottles, place them
under a continuously running
pipe: cars going by fade

in the river, the resonance
of water rises in your jugs
and the pour-like spear from

the spigot fills the lower
frequencies so you hear
your mother's voice, your

father's, as water falls to
the grated drain and flows
to the river and the sound.

6 a.m., The First Job

All this strangeness:
George spading his iron
pole down through myrtle

trying for the septic
tank, morning a light
green covering, 'honey'

truck idling beside
the purple rhododendron,
a honeybee bumping gold

on the window screen,
then, after he shovels
away dirt-loam and hooks

the cement cap up and off,
decades of ocean-sweet
musk flavoring the air.

Roaring Brook: Her Christening

Talk about curving when The Reverend
bent over to touch a palm to her fore-
head, reached out in a human arc
and splashed drops over her white
pinafore, spoke as he curved with his
cupped hand dripping brook-water
that runs church-side down through
Cotton Hollow, said what flows from
gravity welcomes the newborn into
the community and carries the centuries
into a sun-washed Sunday morning and,
if you believe or don't, these are
still waters from which life comes,
still the future in which the past
pours through a glacial-carved gap
of mill ruins, washing over our lives.

As The Years Pass I Almost Forget

how you lurched into the pews
as you staggered down the aisle
under a Bach fugue screaming
"no" to vaulted emptiness
because your brother, a minister,
had had his throat cut in
his living room by a man
he'd taken in from the street,

how we gathered in the parlor
afterwards to offer solace
and to share roast turkey,
quiche, and five soups,

how, a week later in your
restaurant, a vase of white
roses had been placed in
each hand-decorated booth
and the kitchen went on cooking
Mexican, Italian, plain
old-fashioned people's food.

I knew, then, your restaurant
would remain your life, that
you would carry in arm-loads of
lettuce day after day as you
do this afternoon when you
bump my booth and I remember
how you got down the aisle
because a friend put his arm around
your waist under the organ-thunder
attempting to lift you back to life.

Tides In Auke Bay

All of the peninsula ebbs:
the bay, creek, and river,
the heron who beats slowly

down mud-flats to open
water, an eagle who banks
for a surface-catch before

flying to dozens drying out
in a sun-lit patch of air.
Even the mussels which cling

to boulders in clamped-shut
intelligence tighten and with-
draw. Spent king crab shells

slide and settle on a beach-
litter of brown and gray.
A raven with her croaked 'Gaa'

jumps down through old-man's-
hair hanging mist-pure on
a sitka spruce. A seal's eyes

close in a whirlpool hunger
with salmon and herring
beneath and beneath them

the understanding of sea-
floor, mud, and continental
plate on which the flood will

60

sweep kelp and plankton up
to glacial spill as everything is
informed and measured by tides.

On The 'Adventure Bound' Going To A Fiord

When the fluke appears then disappears
Aisha doesn't believe she's seen it

and plants herself by the bow rail
going by Taku Inlet and the running-

down snow-melt over talus rock-fall.
She wants certainty about what the skipper

says just surfaced, a humpback, so
she curls her knuckles round stainless

steel and hunts an answer to her deep
question before she looks for sea lion,

orca, or one of the other animals
these low-achieving kids from Dallas

are here for, what wild Alaska might
give them months or years later, braves

the twenty-knot wind and stares out
at the fiord, the two Detroit diesels

purring spray into a trailing wake
until, as the distances of sheer cliff

rise into the junction of rock-mass
and mist, the skipper throttles down,

calls muffled over the one working
speaker, "For those who've played

62

against bears there's one off port,
gorged with mussels after waking from

a long sleep." But Aisha's watching
the water, insistent that she know

beyond all doubt before she goes on
to the next question, though all her

friends run to port to see the black
bear climbing around a rock, Aisha on

the bow looking for a whirlpool, for
whale, while the bear goes haunch up

and looks at them not a hundred yards
away before disappearing into greening

alder, Aisha gripping the rail while
the kids tumble into the cabin and peel

off their black Desert Hawk parkas,
her eyes opened into distance and closed

inwards on the further distance of
truth as she insists on knowing what's

real in this surge-turning fiord,
the wild domain of growing things,

because she'd discovered, even before
coming here, something to care about.

Homeless

A man opened his hotel
door and walked naked in
front of me to the shower,
all grizzled and gnarled
from years in the bush,
thin legged with uncut
gray hair to his shoulders.
He'd hung his towel on
his right forearm as if
he were going to a ballroom
and the TV sounded through
his open door with low cut
quiz-show voices as his bare
feet sponged the scarlet,
gold-trecked and mildewed
carpet before he went in-
to the bath. Then he was
singing some tune out of
the old days in Cork where
he came from through Canada
to Alaska, his voice smoked
Irish in its almost tenor
with water trickling over
his shoulders like a water-
fall plunging down moss
and crevassed diorite in
some Alaska fiord, a tune
transposing into the hoarse
rise of Danny Boy which
he falls into when he gets
to the end of his days all

gnarled and beaten through,
to the day and night in
an hotel he's given once
a month where he plays
the TV all night and steps
almost stately, bone-thin
naked, back to his room
four times a day after
bathing in anonymous water.

Candlelight Dinner By The Harbor

Your father, missing in action
in Viet Nam thirty years ago,
hovers in words above deep

fried halibut and crab fresh
from the seas around Sitka,
hovers below the North Pacific

map beside the restaurant
window where sleet and wind
buffet the glass, weather

come northeast up from Hainan,
Taiwan, the Aleutians, a low
swept over seas, sea-mammals,

life-links. You, by coming to
Alaska, found your calling as
a minister but not your dad,

by coming west to the continent's
edge found a new wife though
not your dad, found your second

calling as a writer and poet
though never your dad. What's
left of him lies further, maybe

in mountains or a Vietnam
village, maybe in the South
China Sea where west becomes

east far beyond this window
and flickering grill beside
which you recall an Air Force

pilot from back east, his
brown-eyed Kentucky child-
hood overlooking trawlers

and seiners harbored under
rain and January snow, what
words and a map summon of

the broken desires of sonhood,
a father above the halibut
that blesses us as we eat.

Passage To Glacier Bay

Here where the tides ebb and flow
   twenty feet a day and where a spring
      night barely falls into what isn't even

darkness but a pale mellow glow
   under clouds, where the almost sinister
      whisper of rain mists spruce and hemlock

and a creek plunges through muskeg
   off a rock face, I reach out dreaming
      before dawn to touch you but feel only empty

sheets, empty bed, turn on
   the light and read how the Inupiat
      flow and meld with long Arctic nights, with

the weather when horizons disappear
   and distances turn over into the clarity
      of what seems near and, in the middle of

that flowing with them, in
   the middle of the tides, I remember
      what I was pulled awake by, me dreaming I

was in the waiting room when
   you were going under for a biopsy.
      I hadn't told you my terror on the drive to

the hospital because I wanted
   to be strong to give you strength.
      So, when we learned you were clear, my relief

swept away my fear and carried
     me into the deep present, though
          your relief brought you someplace I could

only imagine, maybe the place
     I've come to way beyond that waiting
          room with its plastered-white fluorescence

as I learn how the Inupiat in a far
     away night seine sunrise and sunset
          into near flowing distances even when

warmth and light are almost not,
     how the ebb on the mussel-littered
          beach below this cabin carries away fear

and the pale flood of not quite
     darkness and leaves the sound of
          a muskeg-brown waterfall trickling into the tides.

III

The Green Flooded Hollows Of This Mesa

Promises

An ice-locked January
brook coming down from
Cuchina Peak above Taos:
water slips under snow
covered plates where one
soap-shimmering bubble
after another slowly
percolates and slides
away, where fire-blackened
ponderosa from a blow-
up two years ago stand
quiet in grace, where
someday overhung bank-
ice will drip and shine
and draw down winter,
where saplings will green
charred ground and a lack-
luster May morning will
melt in a fierce course
of boulders, where creek-
ice on this windless
mountain offers a few
notes of piped-organ
hollow water and holds
the bedrock of spring.

Burial: Arroyo Seco

Celestino is saying quietly
that his great grandfathers
dug the acequias with oxen

two hundred years ago as he
ratchets open a come-along
to pull a friend's dead mare

onto an unhitched, back-gate-
lifted flat-bed to drive to
the landfill, chains her hind

legs and says water courses
the ditches when there's enough
snow-melt but this year new

landowners are angry because
of the drought, then, after he
connects the chain to the come-

along and gets purchase on
her well-beyond half-ton body,
thumbs his blue-striped grain-

cap, says his father in his day
moved sheep from this winter
pasture up through Hondo

Canyon for summer grazing.
The come-along goes click,
click and the mare slips for-

ward, her forelegs like pegs
or two angled two-by-fours
stuck sideways in the ground.

When they catch on the bed's
steel fence he nooses a rope
around her neck and legs, ties

the bitter end to the chain
to bring her fore-legs upright
and her head. The day's easy

with death and Celestino's
talk and the lateral acequia
runs half full as the pulley

and rope bend her neck to
the sky so that she watches
the world. After we drop

the cup on the hitch-tongue
and slip the cotter-pin through,
Celestino whispers, "she ran

the green-flooded hollows of
this mesa, that's why she's
looking," then drives gently

over the culvert-bridged water.

Riding Down The El Salto Road

His son screams, 'fucking-
truck,' and brings a .22
out of the aluminum-roofed
trailer, kicks the tire of
an acetylene-torched back-
bed of what was once a pale
blue pickup, sharp bright
shards of his voice, then
Celestino's voice, 'Oh,
get to work,' as he picks
up beer cans and wrappings.
The night before I sat with
him on his front steps:
A clear night disappearing
into fog when he told me
how three years ago he'd
ridden home on horseback
in a storm, woke up lying
in his backyard and didn't
remember the lightning,
how the saddle came down
on his face. Cheek bones
replaced by titanium, his
mouth wired shut for six
months so he had to eat
hamburgers through a straw.
Face 'bionic' now, all new,
he laughed proudly. Life-Star
had helicoptered him down
the Rio to Albuquerque
while he clung to its wooden

gurney because he wanted
a lifeboat so scared he
was of crashing in the gorge.
His son yells again, fires
three times at an apple
tree beside the backbed
before cradling the .22
and Celestino's holding
on for dear life, holding
the lifeboat he doesn't have.

Pastures Awaiting Subdivision

The cedar-fanned windmill
on the Torres Hacienda still
turns for water and though

the ranch raises Carolais,
a super breed of cattle,
and the decades-old tractor

pops and backfires when it
sets posts for new fence,
the white clavicle and skull

over the gate say nobody wants
this ranch after the Padre
dies and the orange-ribboned

stakes on the corners of
the pasture announce that water
will stop running the ditches,

heifers no longer come to
the loading gate, though in
the window at night when

lightning knocks out lamps
in the living room, the hall-
way, and the sodium flood-

light by the barn, candle-
light reaches the acequia
madre dug generations ago,

even as the tan, soft marble
fireplace flashes thunder-
white in a mountain storm.

For Barbara, On The Death Of Her Horse

Earth, we gave you footpaths and walked
beside
the mountain. We bridled our dreams

and they fell: the ground lay
heavy
with bones. Then Barbara came

and the morning. She placed a wild
iris
on the ear of Ginger who had returned

to you, the magpies cackling,
not yet
plunging for her eyes. She knelt

and put a hand on her white forehead
and you
cradled her when she heard hoofbeats.

Words For A Friend With Prostate Cancer

Colder but wiser oh still
green heart be with me, be
as seasons keep renewal

and the earth its rhythms,
be as the seed that sleeping
through winter draws in sun

and water. Stay through my fear.
Be my faith as this hand
traces what it cannot touch,

a word sprung from my warm
blood before returning, a voice
as it was from the beginning.

Frank, You Taught Us All

An oceanic voice within
recalls the vast eyes
of your blue belief so
perfectly and sweetly

gathered into speech:
consummate, the depths
of sound from which
your standards for tone

and sentence rose no
higher than what you
were and were for us
our measure, my memory

of your five-foot two-
inch frame summing
"The Pardoner's Tale"
or Satan's magnificent

stupidity, the words
you loved and spoke,
"silly" meaning close
to God, "kind" our

nature, your greeting
on the phone always,
"Frank Quinn here,"
then the brogueish

laugh teaching us
how we learn "a this
and that" followed by
your bell-clear voice

rung from the soul,
tiding sure-timbered
Scottish strength
afloat on history.

Near The Granite Stone In The Aspen Grove

Your widow's kept your '66 Galaxy
two door under a tarp the six
years you've been dead. Didn't
even put it on blocks to protect

the bearings, let alone wash it.
Birds and dirt daubers have built
nests in the engine block, mice
and chipmunks in the upholstery.

One day she had the battery taken
out of her Toyota and put in
the Galaxy, had her friend turn
the key – when the engine didn't

catch she leaned on the hood, bent
her body into valves and pistons,
rods and rings, the film of her
flowered, lily-pond gown pressed

against the wheel well till she
became transparent, blended with
time in the silent monotone that
looks down on grief, your car in

the rust-red color she couldn't
part with, that wouldn't start
again ever, as much a part of
what she wasn't as what she was.

Below The Medicine Wheel

Long dumb voices
   tumbling over the empty roads
      of Wyoming. I didn't go further west after

I heard them
   because the canyon stayed
      in my head for days, a twisted concourse of rock

where a stream-
   funnel poured onto bottom land,
      sheer-fall cliffs, a plate of earth decaved into

burial depressions,
   a woman's voice, a man's, flute-
      vibrations from two-hundred-year-old cottonwoods

leaning over to die.
   It wasn't them or the petroglyphs
      black-gnashed in the cliff sides but the uplift

rock itself,
   within it, something beyond depth,
      something underneath the owls hooded-over their

swift--drawn wings,
   underneath stick-shadowed bow
      and arrow men, armless hands and legless feet.

Even the river-water
   didn't cause them, gurgles in a wash
      of keys beside which piles of femur and thigh-bones

lay under the cindered
    protection of the rock face.
        The sounds were the sounds of mountain and land,

from toothed holes
    and death's-heads spilling out
        strings and curlicues of brain, all the instruments

through which
    earth speaks, not just the tearing-
        away ground and wind but pipe-sounds, earth-

language tumbling
    inside me, the cry of a horned
        figure dancing with one arm up and the other down.

Winter Feast Day, The Pueblo

A January sun across the sky's
bowl, earth drumbeats coursing

the plaza and moving from
the South House to the North,

ladders from roof-door to
roof, the frozen creek bed,

morning, afternoon, evening,
a bobcat skin keeping time

beside a white shawled woman
with rattle shells on her

wrists, a child with two
eagle feathers tied to each

shoulder, ice-cold air warmed
by friction between earth

and sky, buffalo stomping
between two adobe buildings

out to the plaza as drums
counter other drums that lead

the lead dancer's shaggy
buffalo head down and up,

his blood-red eye, other
white-streaked faces, five

deer, other buffalo, ankle
bells above underground drum

sticks on tanned hides, frozen
dust, feet-stamping ground

become what it is: earth-
mind which no one enters or

leaves because one is always
there, beat of knowledge-

filled knowing, cut mountains
bringing spring to winter,

ever-green drums carving
creeks, rivers, a high elk antler

the eye of an eagle unmoved
and moving before the main

adobe house as the swirl of
dirt-frost carries, is carried

into, leg bone, spine, skull,
tendons sprung by the herds

we feast on, that feast on us
in the earth-rocked-bowl of dance.

IV

In This Vault

Beyond, Behind The Totems, January 2003, Sitka National Historic Park

In this vault of second growth,
Haida Watchmen and Raven don't
speak but spruce, hemlock, do.

At low tide they say: "Grow as
we grow in this nave where each
ring is the years' holy word, each

needle and frond your scripture.
Trunks and boughs rise from pews
of nurse logs for the wind to hymn.

From pulpits of decay and parasites
we speak the only text there is,
here where all aisles lead to

ground, where root-columns lift
mineral, mist, and dregs of salmon-
flesh to buttress all family trees,

where swinging boughs drip with
pure decay and smell of the future,
where what's altered is rain turned

into mold and woody strength, now,
with your culture, about to go
to war, commit murder, know your

immemorial ancestry rooted in
ceremonies of stone and rain: this
grove, this grave, this comfort."

NOTES

"Buying Firewood"	for Ray Shorey
"Purging New Cylinders After A Two Foot Snow"	for Bob & Jeannine Sahagen
"Preservation"	for Olive and James Turner
"Bringing A Fir Straight Down"	for Bob Frazer
"Bending Steel"	for Russell House
"Care"	for Bruce Trundy
"Occurrences"	for Ernie van Soeren
"Roaring Brook: Her Christening"	for my Granddaughter, Amelia Ruth Packard
"As The Years Pass I Almost Forget"	for Timothy Otte
"Tides In Auke Bay"	for Ellen & Alan Rogers
"Candlelight Dinner By The Harbor"	for Jim Drury
"Passage To Glacier Bay"	for Kathryn Kelly
"For Barbara, On The Death Of Her Horse"	for Barbara Waters
"Words For A Friend With Prostate Cancer"	for Nate Bolls
"Frank, You Taught Us All"	for Frank Quinn
"Near The Granite Stone In The Aspen Grove"	for Frank Waters

About the Author

Hugh Ogden is the author of three books of poems (most recently, *Gift)* and two chapbooks. Among his awards are a National Endowment For The Arts Fellowship and three grants from the Connecticut Commission On The Arts. He's been a Fellow at the MacDowell Colony twice and won residencies at The Island Institute, Hawthorden Castle, The Château de Lavigny, and other artist colonies. He's taught at Trinity College for 38 years where he co-founded the Creative Writing program. He also founded the Creative Writing Program at the Academy For The Arts in Hartford (a magnet high school) where he teaches poetry workshops. Before coming to Trinity, he taught for 7 years at the University of Michigan in the Honors Program. He and his partner, Kathryn Kelly, live in Glastonbury, CT and, part of the year, on an island in a northwest Maine mountain lake.